AMERICA AT WAR

THE CIVIL WAR
1861–1865

Simon Rose

www.av2books.com

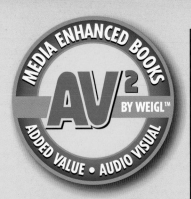

AV² provides enriched content that supplements and complements this book. Weigl's AV² books strive to create inspired learning and engage young minds in a total learning experience.

Your AV² Media Enhanced books come alive with...

Audio
Listen to sections of the book read aloud.

Key Words
Study vocabulary, and complete a matching word activity.

Go to www.av2books.com, and enter this book's unique code.

Video
Watch informative video clips.

Quizzes
Test your knowledge.

BOOK CODE

Z176756

Embedded Weblinks
Gain additional information for research.

Slide Show
View images and captions, and prepare a presentation.

AV² by Weigl brings you media enhanced books that support active learning.

Try This!
Complete activities and hands-on experiments.

... and much, much more!

Published by AV² by Weigl
350 5th Avenue, 59th Floor
New York, NY 10118
Websites: www.av2books.com   www.weigl.com

Library of Congress Cataloging-in-Publication Data
Rose, Simon.
 Civil War / Simon Rose.
   pages cm. -- (America at war)
 Includes index.
 ISBN 978-1-4896-1554-1 (hardcover : alk. paper) -- ISBN 978-1-4896-1555-8 (softcover : alk. paper) -- ISBN 978-1-4896-1556-5 (ebk.) -- ISBN 978-1-4896-1557-2 (ebk.).
 1. United States--History--Civil War, 1861-1865--Juvenile literature. I. Title.
 E468.R79 2014
 973.7--dc23
                          2014017526

Printed in the United States of America in North Mankato, Minnesota
1 2 3 4 5 6 7 8 9 0 18 17 16 15 14

052014
WEP310514

Editor: Heather Kissock
Design: Mandy Christiansen

Photograph Credits
We acknowledge Getty Images, Corbis, Newscom, Alamy, and iStockphoto as our primary photo suppliers.

Every reasonable effort has been made to trace ownership and to obtain permission to reprint copyright material. The publishers would be pleased to have any errors or omissions brought to their attention so that they may be corrected in subsequent printings.

CONTENTS

America at War

The United States is a country that was born out of conflict. The American Revolutionary War was a fight for independence from **colonial rule**. From 1775 to 1783, colonists fought British rule for the right to forge their own destiny. Their commitment to the cause established the country as a fierce and loyal **ally**. When called upon, the United States has always fought bravely to protect its values and way of life.

While the Civil War was fought throughout what is now the northeast and southeast United States, most of the fighting took place in the states of Virginia and Tennessee.

Since its inception, the United States has been involved in a number of wars and conflicts. These include the War of 1812, the American Civil War, the Mexican-American War, and several battles with American Indians. The United States was also involved in the latter stages of World War I and played a major role in World War II. Since 1945 alone, the United States has taken part in conflicts in Korea, Vietnam, Iraq, and Afghanistan.

No matter how a war ends, it usually leads to changes for both sides of the conflict. On the global scale, borders change, new countries are created, people win their freedom, and **dictators** are deposed. Changes also occur on a national level for almost every country involved.

The United States has experienced great change as a result of war. War has shaped the country's political, economic, and social landscape, making it the country it is today.

The Civil War divided not only the country, but families as well. Depending on where they lived, it was not uncommon to see brothers fighting each other on the battlefield.

A War Begins

The United States had been moving toward a civil conflict for years. Significant differences between the northern and southern states had led to growing tensions within the country. Many of these differences were related to economic development. The North was more industrialized than the South. It had large urban areas, a larger population, and a well-developed **infrastructure** that included roads and railways. The South, on the other hand, was less developed and had slower population growth. Being less industrialized, it relied on agriculture as its primary industry.

Key to the economy of the South was the use of slaves as laborers. Plantation owners could have up to 300 slaves working in their tobacco or cotton fields. Slaves earned little or no money for their work. They survived on the food and shelter provided to them by their owners. The profits made from tobacco or cotton sales belonged to the plantation owner alone.

This arrangement did not sit well with many Northerners, causing bitter disputes between the North and the South. As the United States expanded westward, the issue of slavery became more contested. Southern states wanted slavery to be allowed in any new states or territories that were formed. Northern states did not. There were also disputes over the rights of the individual states in relation to federal control. By 1861, the situation had become so tense that war was inevitable.

Almost 4 million African Americans lived as slaves in the United States in 1860. Most worked on cotton plantations in the South.

The Roots of the Civil War

SLAVERY

After the American Revolution, most northern states abandoned slavery, but it continued to grow in the southern states. Opposition in the North led to the formation of the **abolitionist** movement, which fought to bring an immediate end to slavery. Some of the actions taken were subtle, such as Harriet Beecher Stowe's novel *Uncle Tom's Cabin,* which exposed the cruelty of slavery. Others were more direct, such as John Brown's efforts to start a slave rebellion at Harpers Ferry. Southerners were convinced that the North was trying to outlaw their way of life.

WESTERN EXPANSION

Western expansion in the 19th century created several new territories and states. Fierce debates took place about whether slavery should be permitted in these new territories. The Missouri Compromise of 1820 banned slavery north of 36 degrees. It was not until the Kansas-Nebraska Act of 1854 that individual states were given the right to decide whether to allow or ban slavery. When the slavery issue was put to a vote in Kansas, violence erupted between the two sides. This led to increased tensions between the northern and southern states.

SOUTHERN ALIENATION

The disparity between the North and South in terms of development and population growth led to a feeling of alienation in the South. With its booming economy and growing population, the North held enough power to exert considerable influence over decisions regarding the nation. Southerners felt that they were losing their influence within the U.S. government and that there was no one in the North willing to protect the interests of the South. When the Northerners began to campaign for an end to slavery, Southerners feared the collapse of their economy.

STATE RIGHTS

Southern leaders tried to protect their interests by raising the issue of state rights. This challenged how much authority the federal government should have over the laws of individual states. Southern leaders tried to use state rights to protect slavery. They argued that the federal government had no right to pass laws about slavery in states where it was already in place. They also stated that the government could not stop slaveowners from taking slaves into the new territories. If state rights were not going to be respected, the South was ready to form its own country.

The War Between the States

The Civil War is also known as the War Between the States. The war divided the country into two parts. The northern states were known as the Union, and the southern states were called the Confederacy. There were three main theaters of war. The Eastern Theater included the area north of North Carolina and east of the Appalachian Mountains. The Western Theater covered the area south of Virginia, west of the Appalachians, and east of the Mississippi River. The Trans-Mississippi Theater included the lands west of the Mississippi River.

This map demonstrates the scope of the Civil War and some of the key battles that took place.

Texas

Abraham Lincoln,
President of the United States

Jefferson Davis,
President of the Confederate States

Iowa

Illinois

Indiana

Ohio

Pennsylvania

New Jersey

Gettysburg, 1863 ★

Delaware

Antietam, 1862 ★

Bull Run, 1861, 1862 ★

Maryland

Chancellorsville, 1863 ★

Wilderness, 1864 ★

Spotsylvania, 1864 ★

Virginia

Petersburg, 1864 ★

Missouri

Kentucky

Appomattox, 1865

Fort Henry, 1862 ★

North Carolina

Arkansas

★ **Fort Donelson, 1862**

Tennessee

★ **Stones River, 1863**

Shiloh, 1862 ★

Columbia, 1865 ★

★ **Chickamauga, 1863**

Memphis, 1862 ★

South Carolina

★ **Atlanta, 1864**

Georgia

Fort Sumter, 1861 ★

Vicksburg, 1863 ★

Alabama

Mississippi

Louisiana

★ **New Orleans, 1862**

Florida

Legend

■ Union Army

□ Confederate Army

□ Neutral

★ Major Battle

0   250 Miles

0   250 Kilometers

N

America Goes to War

The increasing power of the northern states meant that it was only a matter of time before a northern, anti-slavery president was elected. This happened in November 1860, when Abraham Lincoln was elected as president of the United States. Lincoln's Republican Party opposed the expansion of slavery in the West, and people in the South feared that Lincoln would abolish slavery altogether. By the end of the year, South Carolina decided to **secede** from the Union. It was soon followed by other southern states. By the time Lincoln took the oath of office in March 1861, seven southern states had left the Union to form the Confederate States of America.

Lincoln's inauguration took place on the steps of the Washington Capitol. The event drew a crowd of about 25,000 people.

Southerners were prepared to fight for their new country, and it was not long before Confederate forces were threatening to attack Fort Sumter in Charleston, South Carolina, which was held by northern troops. Lincoln decided it would be best to send ships to resupply the fort in case the attack went forward. This prompted the Confederate forces to attack before the ships arrived. The first shots of the Civil War were fired on April 12, 1861, and the fort surrendered. Lincoln then ordered a **blockade** for all southern ports and issued a call for 75,000 volunteers to join the army and defeat the rebelling forces. Northern states supplied troops, but Virginia, Arkansas, North Carolina, and Tennessee decided to join the Confederacy.

Soldiers and supplies quickly arrived in Washington, DC, and the Union army was assembled. On July 21, 1861, in the First Battle of Bull Run, 35,000 Confederate troops led by Thomas "Stonewall" Jackson defeated a much larger Union force. The Union Army was forced to retreat toward the capital. Northern leaders were shocked by the defeat, and Lincoln called for another 500,000 men. It became clear to both sides that the war would be long and costly.

Abraham Lincoln
The 16ᵗʰ U.S. President

Abraham Lincoln was born in Kentucky in 1809. He later lived in Indiana and Illinois. Lincoln was elected to the Illinois Legislature in 1825. He then became a lawyer and was elected to the U.S. Congress for one term in 1845. Lincoln ran unsuccessfully for a seat in the Senate in 1858. During the campaign, he voiced his opposition to slavery.

Lincoln was elected as president in 1860. The Civil War started shortly after he took office. Lincoln faced many challenges during the war, but he was determined to keep the country together. During the war, Lincoln gave a memorable speech known as the Gettysburg Address. In this speech, he referred to the Civil War as a struggle not only to preserve the Union but also to bring freedom and equality to all Americans and ensure the survival of **democracy**.

When the conflict ended in April 1865, Lincoln wanted to reconcile with the southern states and help them to rebuild. He was assassinated before he could put his plans in motion. Lincoln died on April 15, 1865, at the age of 56.

One of Lincoln's best-known accomplishments as president was the Emancipation Proclamation of 1863, which freed all slaves living in rebelling states.

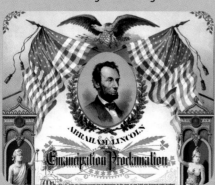

The Lincoln Memorial was built to honor Lincoln and his contributions to the country. It was unveiled on May 22, 1920 at the west end of the National Mall in Washington, DC.

Americans Who Served in the Civil War

Most of the men who enlisted to fight in the Civil War became soldiers in the Union or Confederate Armies. Some, however, were sailors. These men served on boats stationed on rivers in the West or on ships that enforced the Union blockade of southern ports. Women also played an active role in the war. Most were nurses, but hundreds secretly joined the Army and fought on both sides in some of the war's bloodiest battles.

Union Soldiers

The men who fought for the Union were between 18 and 45 years of age, with an average age of about 26. Most of the men who enlisted came from the agricultural community. However, the ranks of the Union Army also included accountants, teachers, shoemakers, painters, blacksmiths, and a number of other occupations. Approximately one quarter of Union Army soldiers were immigrants, and about 10 percent were African Americans. The rest were native-born white Americans.

At the beginning of the war, regular Union soldiers were paid $13 per month, while African Americans were paid $10 per month. In June 1864, this amount increased to $16. This increase applied to regular soldiers and any African American troops that had been free men before the war. Former slaves did not receive the increase.

A soldier's life was not always exciting. When not fighting, soldiers spent their time writing letters, playing card games, and making music.

Confederate Soldiers

Like the Union soldiers, those in the Confederate Army were, on average, 26 years of age. Most soldiers were native-born white Southerners from farming backgrounds, but other professions included carpenters, mechanics, merchants, teachers, and lawyers. Exact numbers are unknown, but tens of thousands of foreign-born soldiers are also believed to have fought for the Confederacy.

The Confederate Army was not always well armed. In the Second Battle of Bull Run, they had to throw rocks at the enemy when their ammunition ran out.

When the war began, Confederate soldiers were paid $11 per month. This was raised to $18 per month in the summer of 1864, but by that time the Confederate currency had dropped sharply in value, and the money did not go very far. While soldiers were given **rations**, these supplies decreased in the later months of the war. The soldiers tried to live off the land, but many were starving by the end of the war.

United States Colored Troops

African American men who wanted to fight for the Union were placed in United States Colored Troops (USCT) regiments. Some African American recruits worked in the **infantry** as foot soldiers and **cavalry**. Others worked in **artillery** units. In total, 180,000 African Americans served in 163 units during the last two years of the war. They accounted for about 10 percent of all troops who fought in the Civil War.

About 18,000 men and more than a dozen women served in the navy during the war. They made up about 15 percent of the total enlisted naval force.

Sailors

When the war began, the Union had a navy consisting of fewer than 40 ships. This was still more than the Confederacy, however, which had no navy at all. The only ships available to it were its small **merchant marine** fleet. Both sides set to work at increasing their naval forces, building ships and recruiting men to defend their waters.

Men who joined the Union Navy were usually from the working classes. Some were immigrants or former slaves. While most joined for money, others believed that the Navy would be safer than the Army and have better conditions. Sailors who served on blockade ships led a hard and often boring life, as they were typically restricted to the ship and forced to work long hours. On the rivers, men often faced dangerous situations. Confederate **snipers** operating from the shore would shoot at Union boats and their crew as they patrolled the rivers. If the ship's engines were shattered during battle, the sailors could be horribly scalded and disfigured by the hot steam.

Some Confederate ships, such as the *Sumter*, *Alabama*, and *Shenandoah*, served as commerce raiders. They would attack Union merchant ships at sea. These ships usually had Confederate **officers** but foreign crews.

The naval battles of the Civil War extended far beyond the North American coastline. In 1864, the English Channel was the site of a battle between the Union ship *Kearsarge* and the Confederate ship *Alabama*.

Women in the War

While most women watched over the home during the war, some decided they wanted to be part of the action. In June 1861, Dorothea Dix was appointed as superintendent of Union Army nurses. She helped to recruit nurses, set up training programs, and establish field hospitals and first-aid stations. More than 3,000 women were recruited as nurses. Many others cared for the wounded as volunteers. One of the best-known nurses of the Civil War was Clara Barton, who later founded the American Red Cross. In the South, women often took wounded soldiers into their homes and provided care for them there.

Louisa May Alcott, the author of *Little Women*, served as a nurse in the Civil War. She later wrote a book on nursing called *Hospital Sketches*.

Hundreds of women also disguised themselves as men and joined the army. Their true identities were rarely discovered unless they were wounded, sick, or captured. Among the many women who fought in the war were Sarah Edmonds, who enlisted in the Second Michigan Infantry as Franklin Thompson, Frances Clayton, who served in Missouri artillery and cavalry units as Jack Williams, and Loreta Velazquez, who fought for the Confederacy under the name Harry Buford.

One of the best-known women fighters was Bridget Devens, also known as Michigan Bridget. She served with the Union's First Michigan Cavalry. When not fighting, she tended to the wounded in the field.

A Soldier's Uniform

Soldiers in the Union and Confederate Armies wore similar uniforms. Union uniforms were dark blue, and most Confederate uniforms were gray. Both Union and Confederate soldiers were equipped with a standard uniform that they wore while on active duty in the field. Each soldier also had a kit that accompanied the uniform. The kit contained all the equipment the soldier was expected to need while away from camp. The soldier carried his gear wherever he went.

CAP

Both sides had two types of wool caps, called the forage and the kepi. The caps provided shade in the summer, warmth in the winter, and protected the soldier from rain. Most of the caps had a leather brim, sweatband, and an adjustable chinstrap with a brass slide. Forage caps had a narrow leather visor, a high crown, and a round, flat top that flopped forward. The kepi's top tilted at less of an angle and had a lower crown. Confederate caps varied in color depending on which branch of the army the soldier was serving in.

JACKET

Jackets were made of wool and kept the soldier warm in the winter. They could be very hot in the summer, however. Regular soldiers and infantry officers wore a single-breasted jacket that extended to the middle of the thigh. High-ranking officers wore double-breasted jackets. Buttons and other **insignia** indicated the soldier's rank and the branch to which he belonged.

TROUSERS

A soldier's trousers were made of wool and usually matched the jacket. A stripe down the outside of the leg indicated the branch of the military to which the soldier belonged. A yellow stripe meant he was in the cavalry, while a dark blue stripe showed he was an infantry soldier. A soldier with a red stripe on his trousers was a member of the artillery.

FOOTWEAR

Soldiers mostly wore lace-up shoes with a high ankle and up to six eyelets for laces. These shoes were called bootees or ankle boots and had a square toe. The shoes were made of black leather that was smooth on the outside. The quality of a Union soldier's shoes was usually far superior to the shoes of a Confederate soldier.

HAVERSACK

Soldiers carried their rations in their haversack. The haversack was made of canvas. It included a waterproof lining and had a buckled flap. Its strap was slung over the soldier's right shoulder so that the bag itself rested on his left hip. Union haversacks were usually of higher quality than those used by the Confederate side.

KNAPSACK

Soldiers carried their personal belongings in their knapsacks. Items could include a blanket, mess equipment, toilet articles, a sewing kit, a pocketknife, and a small, makeshift shelter called a "dog tent." Knapsacks were made of cotton cloth or canvas and were painted black to make them waterproof.

CARTRIDGE BOX

The cartridge box held the soldier's ammunition. The box held 40 cartridges and had a small pouch for the soldier's cleaning kit. Union soldiers carried between 60 and 80 rounds of ammunition. Extra cartridges were carried in the haversack or in the soldier's pockets. The cartridge box was made of black leather and had a removable tin liner. Its strap was placed over the soldier's left shoulder so that the box rested on his right hip.

CANTEEN

Soldiers carried water in a canteen. This comprised two pieces of tin, a spout made of pewter, and a cork. The canteen was usually carried on the soldier's left side, on top of his haversack. It was often covered with a wet cloth to help keep the water cool.

Weapons of War

Soldiers in the Civil War used a variety of **ballistics**, ranging from rifles and pistols to cannons. New technological improvements made many of these weapons much more lethal than those used in previous wars. The number of Civil War battle **casualties** was high as a result. New advances in naval warfare also had an effect on the way battles were fought. Ironclad ships saw widespread use, and the first submarines were employed. Balloons also made their first appearance in American warfare. They were released into the air to observe enemy positions from above.

RIFLES

Both sides in the Civil War relied on the Springfield rifle musket, although some other models were also carried. The Springfield weighed about 10 pounds (4.5 kilograms) and was a single shot, muzzle-loading gun. It had a rifled barrel and fired the .58 caliber Minié ball bullet. This type of bullet was designed to expand when moving along the rifle barrel. This increased the weapon's muzzle velocity and range. The Springfield could be reloaded quickly and was considered to be very accurate and reliable.

PISTOLS AND REVOLVERS

Colts and Remingtons were the preferred handguns for both Union and Confederate soldiers during the war, although these types of weapons were only effective at close range. The most popular revolvers were six-shooters. These guns were known for their rapid fire and reliability. They also could be reloaded quickly when needed.

ARTILLERY

A number of different cannons were used in the Civil War. Each was classified by the weight of shot used. Light artillery could be set up quickly in the field to support cavalry or infantry units. Weapons included 6-pounder (2.7 kilograms) guns and 12-pounder (5.4 kg) howitzers. Guns were used to fire directly at the enemy, and howitzers were used to fire over their heads. Both types of cannon had wooden carriages with large wheels and were pulled by a team of four or six horses. A team of six or seven soldiers was responsible for setting up, loading, and firing the cannons. The larger guns that comprised heavy artillery had loads ranging from 18 to 42 pounds (8.2 to 19.1 kg). Due to their weight, they were usually located in fixed defensive positions to protect cities or ports.

SUBMARINES

Submarines were used by both Confederate and Union forces during the war. The submarines of the time were metal tubes measuring 4 feet (1.2 meters) across and 40 feet (12.2 m) long. They held a crew of eight. The Confederate vessel CSS *H. L. Hunley* carried out the first successful submarine attack in February 1864. Although it sank a Union blockade ship, the submarine itself was also wrecked during the attack.

IRONCLADS

Ironclads were steam-powered warships that had iron armor plates instead of wooden framing. The ships were slow and difficult to maneuver. However, after the war, the era of wooden ships was over as warships around the world began to be built of iron and steel.

BALLOONS

Both sides used aerial weapons during the war in a limited way. Hydrogen-powered balloons were used to gather **reconnaissance** on the enemy's location. Carrying up to five people at a time, they were deployed over enemy camps and artillery. The balloons often carried a telegrapher who sent information about the enemy to home camp.

Timeline

The War on the Battlefield

April 12, 1861
Confederate forces attack Fort Sumter in Charleston, South Carolina.

April 25, 1862
Union forces capture New Orleans.

August 28 to 30, 1862
The Confederates defeat the Union Army in the Second Battle of Bull Run.

April 6 to 7, 1862
The Union Army defeats Confederate forces at the Battle of Shiloh.

July 21, 1861
The Union Army is defeated at the First Battle of Bull Run.

The War at Home

November 6, 1860
Abraham Lincoln is elected president of the United States.

September 17, 1862
A Union victory at the Battle of Antietam halts Robert E. Lee's invasion of the North.

October 19, 1864
The Union Army defeats Confederate forces at the Battle of Cedar Creek in the Shenandoah Valley.

June 6, 1862
At the Battle of Memphis, Union naval forces defeat the Confederates to secure control of the Mississippi River.

July 1, 1863
The Confederate Army is defeated at the Battle of Gettysburg in Pennsylvania.

April 9, 1865
Lee surrenders his Confederate Army to Ulysses S. Grant at Appomattox Court House in Virginia.

January 1, 1863
President Lincoln issues the Emancipation Proclamation.

April 14, 1865
Abraham Lincoln is shot by John Wilkes Booth. Lincoln dies early the next day.

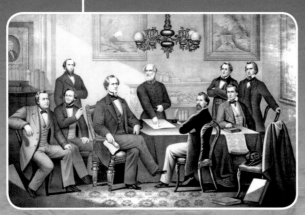

February 9, 1861
The Confederate States of America is founded with Jefferson Davis as president.

Key Battles

The Civil War was the bloodiest conflict in U.S. history. More than 200,000 Americans were killed in battle, and deaths from both sides totalled more than 620,000. Fighting took place across the United States. Some of the war's largest battles claimed more than 20,000 casualties. The Battle of Gettysburg alone claimed more than 50,000 lives.

The Battle of Shiloh was named for the Shiloh Meeting House, a Methodist church that sat on the battlefield. A reconstruction of the church was built in 2001.

Battle of Shiloh

In early 1862, Union General Ulysses S. Grant captured Tennessee's Fort Henry and Fort Donelson, forcing Confederate General Albert Sidney Johnston and his army to retreat from western Tennessee. Grant set up the headquarters for his army of 42,000 men at Pittsburg Landing, on the Tennessee River. He then waited for reinforcements, commanded by Major General Don Carlos Buell, to arrive. Once they were in place, the plan was to attack the city of Corinth, a major railway hub for the Confederacy in northern Mississippi.

Johnston knew he had to protect Corinth at all costs. He decided to attack Grant's army before Buell arrived. On April 3, Johnston and 45,000 Confederate troops left Corinth and made camp close to Pittsburg Landing. Early on April 6, Johnston and his troops launched their attack.

APRIL 3

General Johnston leaves Corinth and leads his Confederate Army toward the camp of Union General Ulysses S. Grant.

APRIL 6

Johnston launches his attack on Grant's army. By the end of the day, the Confederate forces have pushed the Union Army out of an area called the Hornet's Nest.

The Confederate forces took the Union camps by surprise. While some Union troops were forced to give ground, others were able to establish a strong defensive position in an area called the Hornet's Nest. The fight for the Hornet's Nest went on for much of the day. By early evening, however, the Confederate forces had gained the upper hand and pushed the Union line back. While the Union forces were establishing new defensive positions, their reinforcements began to arrive. Grant realized that his forces now outnumbered the Confederates.

Early the next morning, Grant launched a counterattack. By late morning, Union troops had retaken the Hornet's Nest and were moving in on their previous positions at the camps. By mid-afternoon, the Confederate troops accepted that they were outnumbered and began their retreat to Corinth. Most Confederate soldiers had left the battlefield by 5:00 p.m. As his own forces were exhausted, Grant decided not to pursue the enemy. Within weeks, Union forces had renewed their siege on Corinth. They secured the city by the end of May.

Battle of Shiloh

Snake Creek

Buell

Grant

Tennessee River

Owl Creek

Pittsburg Landing

Shiloh Church

Johnston

→ Troops Advancing
--▶ Troops Retreating
■ Union Positions
■ Confederate Positions
— Road

APRIL 7

Grant and his army stage a counterattack. By the end of the day, they have gained back lost ground and forced the Confederates to retreat.

APRIL 7

In two days of fighting, casualties for the Union side total more than 13,000. The Confederates suffer more than 10,000 casualties.

Battle of Antietam

Most of the main battles in the early part of the Civil War had been fought on Confederate territory. However, Confederate President Jefferson Davis believed that a major victory against the Union on northern soil would force Great Britain and France to recognize the Confederacy and help the South's cause. In September 1862, General Robert E. Lee made plans to launch an **offensive** into Maryland and Pennsylvania.

Lee's plans for the invasion were discovered by the Union forces, so they knew exactly how Confederate troops were to be deployed and when actions were to be taken. Despite this knowledge, Union commander General George McClellan was cautious in his pursuit of Lee, even though he had 75,000 soldiers compared to Lee's 38,000.

After leading his troops to several victories, Joseph Hooker was made commander of the Army of the Potomac in 1863.

Early on September 17, Union troops commanded by Joseph Hooker attacked the Confederate left flank, which was positioned west of Antietam Creek. The Confederates were outnumbered, but held their ground until reinforcements arrived. They then counterattacked and drove Hooker's forces back. Support arrived from other Union troops. They made some progress but were eventually forced back by Confederate soldiers. Attacks and counterattacks continued, and by midday, there was a large gap in the Confederate lines. However, McClellan believed that Lee had more than 100,000 soldiers at Antietam and decided not to commit his own 25,000 reserves.

SEPTEMBER 15

Confederate soldiers begin to march into position near Antietam Creek in preparation for the battle to come.

SEPTEMBER 17

Union troops, led by Joseph Hooker, attack the Confederate left flank. After battling back and forth, the Union is able to create a gap in the Confederate lines.

While Hooker was dealing with the Confederate's left flank, Union General Ambrose Burnside attacked the right flank. Lee's forces managed to hold out until General Ambrose Hill arrived with reinforcements and halted Burnside's attack. With the fighting facing a stalemate, McClellan decided not to bring in the rest of his forces. Despite heavy losses, Lee continued to attack on September 18, but moved his wounded back across the Potomac and began to organize his retreat. Although he had more men, McClellan was once again cautious and allowed Lee to escape back to Virginia.

The Battle of Antietam was the bloodiest single day in American history, with more than 22,000 casualties. Neither side could really claim victory, although the Union saw the battle as a success because Lee had been forced to retreat. In the weeks following the battle, President Lincoln removed McClellan as the Union commander and replaced him with Burnside.

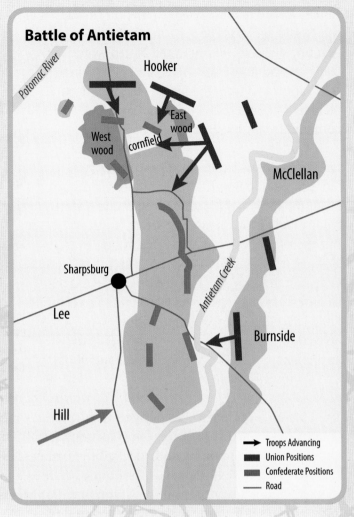

Battle of Antietam

Potomac River

Hooker

East wood

West wood

cornfield

McClellan

Sharpsburg

Antietam Creek

Lee

Burnside

Hill

→ Troops Advancing
▬ Union Positions
▬ Confederate Positions
— Road

SEPTEMBER 17

Union General Ambrose Hill and his army attack the Confederate right flank. The advance is stopped when Confederate reinforcements arrive.

SEPTEMBER 18

General Lee gathers his wounded and begins his retreat to Virginia. The battle results in more than 22,000 casualties and no clear victor.

Battle of Gettysburg

Robert E. Lee remained determined to invade the North. By May 1863, he firmly believed that one decisive victory in the North would bring an end to the war. This time, his main opposition was George Meade, who had been recently appointed by President Lincoln to command the Union forces.

Lee marched his troops into Pennsylvania in late June, stationing his forces at Gettysburg to await the arrival of Meade's army. Some Union troops had already arrived at Gettysburg, but their numbers were not great enough to ward off a Confederate attack. On July 1, Confederate troops forced the Union defenders to retreat through the town as far as Cemetery Hill. That night, however, more troops arrived for both sides, bringing the totals to approximately 94,000 for the Union and about 72,000 for the Confederates.

In November 1863, President Lincoln visited the site of the Battle of Gettysburg to dedicate the national cemetery created there. The speech he gave later became known as the Gettysburg Address.

With his forces in place, Lee decided to attack the Union defensive positions the next day. The Union forces' line extended from Cemetery Hill to Culp's Hill. Lee split up his army and attacked the Union soldiers on both their left and right flanks. Fighting raged for hours, but the Confederates were only able to make minor advances into the Union line. Both sides suffered heavy losses, and two days of fighting had already resulted in almost 35,000 casualties.

JULY 1

Confederate troops enter Gettysburg and force a small advance group of Union troops back to Cemetery Hill. More Union and Confederate forces arrive in the area that night.

JULY 2

General Lee begins to attack Union defensive positions. Little ground is made, but both sides experience heavy losses.

The focus for much of July 3 was on Culp's Hill. After a seven-hour fight for the Union stronghold, Confederate forces were pushed back. Lee then decided to turn his attention to taking Cemetery Hill. He began the attack with a barrage of artillery fire, and then ordered approximately 15,000 Confederate soldiers, commanded by George Pickett, to attack the heavily fortified Union positions. Known as "Pickett's Charge," this attack was disastrous for the Confederate troops. More than 50 percent of the soldiers were killed or wounded.

On July 4, Lee began his withdrawal and the following day retreated across the Potomac River to Virginia. President Lincoln was disappointed that Meade did not pursue the Confederates, but the battle had been a Union victory. It was also the deadliest battle of the Civil War, with more than 50,000 casualties between the two sides.

While Pickett's troops were able to break into the Union line, they were unable to hold their position and were driven back by Union troops.

JULY 3

Union and Confederate forces fight for control of Culp's Hill and then Cemetery Hill. Confederate forces are unable to break the Union line.

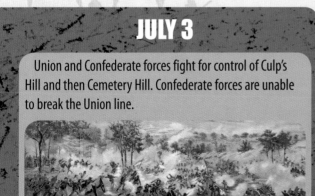

JULY 4

General Lee withdraws what remains of his forces and retreats to Virginia.

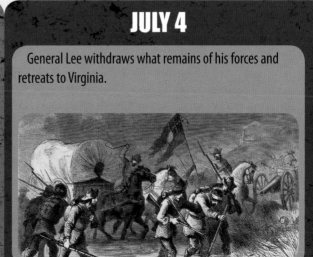

Heroic Americans

The people who served in the Civil War came from a range of backgrounds. Whether they were on the Union or Confederate side, they shared a common desire to fight for their country. While many performed heroic acts, as the war progressed, some names became better known than others. Some soldiers were hailed for their bravery and strong leadership. Others were celebrated because they performed feats unlike anyone else.

ULYSSES S. GRANT (1822-1885)

Ulysses S. Grant was the Union Army's leading commander in the Civil War. He also served as president of the United States from 1869 to 1877.

Grant was born in Ohio in 1822. He attended the U.S. Military Academy at West Point and fought in the Mexican-American War. Grant left the army during the 1850s but rejoined when the Civil War began. His first success of the war came with the capture of Fort Donelson in Tennessee in 1862, after which Grant was promoted to the rank of major general. His capture of Vicksburg in July 1863 split the Confederacy in two. The following year, President Lincoln promoted Grant to general-in-chief of the Union Army. Grant fought Robert E. Lee's forces in Virginia for more than a year before the Confederate surrender in April 1865.

After the war, Grant was elected president in 1868. He served two terms and unsuccessfully ran for a third term in 1880. Grant spent his final years writing his memoirs. These were published just before his death in 1885, at the age of 63.

ROBERT E. LEE
(1807-1870)

Robert E. Lee was the leading commander of the Confederate Army during the Civil War. Although his army lost the war, Lee is considered to be one of America's greatest generals.

Lee was born in Virginia in 1807. He graduated from the U.S. Military Academy at West Point in 1829 and fought in the Mexican-American War alongside Ulysses S. Grant, his future opponent during the Civil War. When the Civil War began, Lee was appointed to command the Confederate Army of Virginia. He led his forces in some of the most important battles of the war, including Gettysburg and Antietam. Confederate forces were often outnumbered, but Lee and his commanders were still able to win several significant victories before the Confederate surrender in April 1865.

Lee later served as president of Washington College in Lexington, Virginia, and supported efforts at reconciliation between the northern and southern states. He died in October 1870, at the age of 63.

WILLIAM TECUMSEH SHERMAN
(1820-1891)

William Tecumseh Sherman was one of the leading generals in the Union Army during the Civil War. He was born in Ohio in 1820 and studied at the U.S. Military Academy at West Point. After serving in the Second Seminole War in Florida in the 1840s, he left the army to pursue a career in banking, and then as a lawyer. Sherman rejoined the military when the Civil War began and was gradually promoted to the rank of major general. Sherman captured Atlanta and led his troops to the port of Savannah during his **March to the Sea**. When Savannah fell on December 21, 1864, Sherman wrote to President Lincoln offering him the city as a Christmas present.

When Grant became president, Sherman was promoted to head of the army in 1869. He retired from the military in 1884. Sherman died in New York City in 1891, at the age of 71.

The Home Front

While soldiers fought on the front lines, other important events were taking place away from the battlefields. People could not escape the fact that the country was at war around them. It impacted them in many ways. The North weathered the war better than the South, where families were subject to many shortages—especially in areas where there was fighting. Women not serving the war effort directly found other ways to help their soldiers, and members of the media tried to keep their communities informed of the war's progress. In fact, the Civil War was one of the first conflicts to be covered on a large scale by the media. Not everyone in the North supported the war effort. There was opposition to **conscription** that resulted in serious riots in New York City in 1863.

The New York Draft Riots

The Enrollment Act of Conscription in March 1863 made all men living in the North between 20 and 45 years of age liable to be drafted into the military. There were only two ways to avoid the draft. One was to find a replacement draftee. The other was to pay the government $300. At that time, $300 was a substantial amount of money. Very few people had that much money on hand. Most had to accept the draft when it came up. The wealthy, however, could just pay the fee and avoid military service. This caused a great deal of resentment. When the federal government tried to enforce conscription in July, riots broke out in several cities in the North. The most serious disturbances took place in New York City. Most of the rioters were poor Irish immigrants. However, instead of taking their frustrations out on government officials, they turned to the city's African American population with whom they competed for jobs. Approximately 100 people were killed, and an African American church and orphanage were burnt to the ground. There was significant damage to property, and President Lincoln had to send troops to the city to restore order.

Besides the estimated 100 people killed during the five days of rioting, more than 100 buildings were burned, with scores of additional injuries, damage to property, and looting.

Women at Home

With so many men away from home serving in the military, women had to work much harder to support their families and keep their farms and businesses in operation. Some women took on their husbands' jobs by plowing fields or managing shops. Others had to find new income from outside sources. They went to work at munitions factories or replaced male workers in government and office positions.

Some women accompanied their husbands to the battlefield. Sometimes bringing their children with them, the women took care of the men by doing laundry and making meals.

As well as working in their new jobs, women on both sides volunteered their time to providing for the troops. They baked, canned food, and grew fruits and vegetables. Women also sewed uniforms, knitted gloves and socks, mended blankets, and ran fundraising campaigns to raise money for medical and other much needed supplies.

African American women faced their own challenges during the war. As Union troops moved into the South, many women had to decide whether to remain where they were or head toward the Union lines and ask for refuge. Those that found themselves behind Union lines were sometimes able to work for the army as hospital aides or seamstresses. Others, however, were unable to find jobs and entered camps specifically set up for former slaves. Here, they tried to survive on gardens and crops they grew themselves.

To protect the home front, some women formed guard units while the men were at war.

The Media

The Civil War was an important era for the development of newspapers. The electric telegraph allowed newspapers to receive reports from the battlefields quickly and report news about victories, defeats, and casualties to the public. Newspaper columnists wrote articles that presented their opinions on aspects of the war. These columns often worked to sway public opinion and encourage debate about the war. *Harper's Weekly* was the most popular publication in both the North and the South during the war. Most of the larger newspapers had reporters in Washington and on the front lines. This allowed them to inform readers about what was happening and why. The Civil War was the first conflict to be photographed on a large scale. Photographs taken of the aftermath of battles had a lasting effect on public opinion during the Civil War.

Even though *Harper's Weekly* was popular in both the North and South, its editorials showed the magazine's support for the Union cause.

Mathew Brady was one of the most important photographers of the Civil War. He and a staff of about 20 went directly to the battlefields to record the events as they occurred.

Sherman's March to the Sea is most remembered for its plunder of communities in the South. His troops were authorized to burn buildings, steal food, and damage railroad lines in an effort to convince Georgia to surrender to the Union.

Hardships in the South

The struggles the South were experiencing before the war began worsened as the war progressed. An economy that was already weak was slowed even further when the Union blockaded ports along the Atlantic coast and in the Gulf of Mexico. The blockades prevented goods from moving in or out of the southern states by sea. This affected businesses that relied on receiving goods from suppliers and shipping goods to customers. The Confederacy's currency steadily became worthless as the fighting continued. Food was also in short supply as a result of the blockades. Supplies that did enter the South were often sent to the Confederate Army rather than the people at home. In April 1863, there were bread riots in Richmond, as women marched to the governor's mansion demanding help. Troops had to be called in to persuade the protestors to go home.

As the South was where most of the fighting took place, families often lived in fear of their homes and farms being overrun by soldiers. When Sherman and his troops moved through Georgia in his March to the Sea, farms, crops, and infrastructure, along with large parts of towns and cities, were destroyed. This caused the local people great hardship.

The War Comes to an End

I n early 1865, the Union Army removed all Confederate resistance from Virginia's Shenandoah Valley. On January 15, 1865, Union forces captured Fort Fisher, North Carolina, the last port under Confederate control. The Union naval blockade and Sherman's March to the Sea the previous fall had caused shortages of food and supplies all over the South. Confederate soldiers began to desert the army. Jefferson Davis authorized the recruitment of slaves, but this did not come into effect until after the war was over.

On February 3, President Lincoln met with Confederate Vice President Alexander Stephens to discuss ending the war. No agreement was reached, and the fighting continued. Sherman had captured Savannah the previous December and was now advancing through South Carolina, destroying anything of value. On February 17, Columbia, South Carolina's capital, was captured. Sherman then headed for Virginia to join other Union forces.

Fort Fisher fell to the Union after a major amphibious attack that used troops from both the army and navy.

More than two thirds of Columbia was destroyed during Sherman's assault on the city. Most of the damage came from fires set by Sherman's troops.

As Lee and Grant met in the house of a local farmer, the Confederate soldiers stood outside with stacked rifles, denoting their surrender to Union forces.

In late March, Lee failed to defeat Grant's forces near Petersburg, Virginia. Confederate forces were then defeated at the Battle of Five Forks on April 1. Union forces were now nearing Richmond, the Confederate capital. Realizing that the Confederate Army would not be able defend the city against the large number of Union troops, Lee abandoned Richmond on April 2, followed closely by President Davis and his government officials. Union troops then moved in and claimed the city.

Lee still hoped to turn the situation around. He began moving his forces south with the hope of amalgamating his remaining troops with Confederate forces in North Carolina. However, his progress was halted by Union soldiers in the Virginia town of Appomattox. Following a brief skirmish, Lee agreed to surrender his forces. On April 9, 1865, he met with Grant at Appomattox Court House in Virginia, where the two men negotiated the terms of surrender. Lee was allowed to keep his sword and his horse, and his soldiers were permitted to return home after surrendering their weapons. Other Confederate forces in the South surrendered when they heard the news. After four long years, the Civil War was over.

The Aftermath

When the war ended, President Lincoln had plans to help the southern states recover. Instead, Andrew Johnson succeeded Lincoln as president and oversaw the period known as Reconstruction. Slavery was abolished, but African Americans still faced severe problems in the decades following the war. The South also continued to face economic and social problems, which caused it to lag behind the North until well into the 20th century.

The Assassination of Lincoln

Only five days after Lee surrendered at Appomattox, President Lincoln was shot while attending a play at Ford's Theatre in Washington. His assailant, actor John Wilkes Booth, was a Southerner who had moved to the North for work. Booth believed that, even though Lee had surrendered, there was still a chance to save the Confederacy. To do this, however, Lincoln had to be killed.

When Lincoln died the next day, the country was thrown into a state of shock. His death also left a void in leadership. This was quickly filled by Vice President Andrew Johnson. However, Johnson was a Southerner who did not have the support of Congress. While Congress wanted to improve the rights of African Americans in the South, Johnson resisted. His efforts to veto new bills in this regard were unsuccessful, and African Americans were afforded more rights and opportunities. After being **impeached** for violating a law, Johnson did not seek a second term.

After shooting President Lincoln, John Wilkes Booth jumped from the balcony to the stage and ran out of the theater. He was captured and shot 12 days later.

The End of Slavery

Slavery was officially abolished in the Thirteenth Amendment to the U.S. Constitution in late 1865. Former slaves became citizens. In subsequent amendments, they received equal protection under the law and the right to vote. Despite these advances, African Americans still faced huge challenges. New laws in the South known as "black codes" restricted the activity of the newly freed slaves. In many states, African Americans had to sign yearly work contracts and could be arrested as vagrants if they refused. Other laws restricted the type of work former slaves could do. White supremacy organizations such as the Ku Klux Klan also impacted the freedom of former slaves. Racism and discrimination in the South would continue long after the Civil War was over.

To escape the restrictions of the black codes, many African Americans packed up their belongings and made their way to the new states in the West.

Reconstruction

Reconstruction is the name given to the rebuilding of the South after the war. This period lasted from 1865 to 1877. One of the first steps the government took was to divide the South into five military districts. This was to prevent another rebellion and to make sure that new laws guaranteeing the end of slavery were put in place. Steps were also taken to improve the quality of life in the South. Roads and farms were rebuilt, and schools were established. Funds were set aside to expand railways into the South and encourage more commerce. Reconstruction efforts gradually declined as governments changed. In the years that followed, many of the Reconstruction ideals were set aside, and the South became racially **segregated** once again.

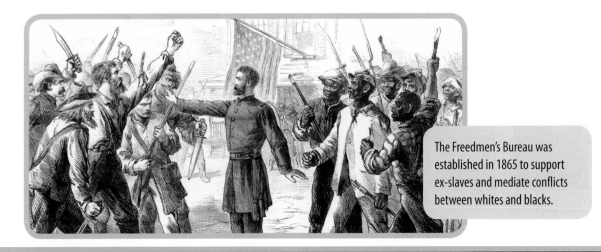

The Freedmen's Bureau was established in 1865 to support ex-slaves and mediate conflicts between whites and blacks.

By The Numbers

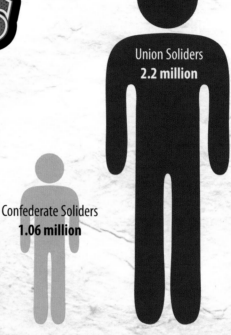

Union Soliders
2.2 million

Confederate Soliders
1.06 million

Civil War Soldiers

During the Civil War, the population of the northern states was more than double that of the southern states. This difference was reflected in the size of the opposing armies, with the Union forces outnumbering the Confederates by about two to one.

North and South

The North had the advantage over the South even before the war started. It had more people, more industry, more skilled workers, and more transportation routes. Economically, it was in a far better position to support its citizens through a war and its aftermath.

■ North

■ South

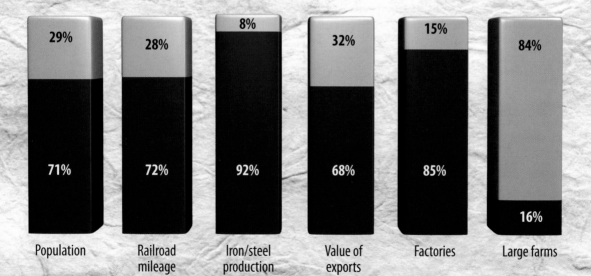

Population	Railroad mileage	Iron/steel production	Value of exports	Factories	Large farms
29%	28%	8%	32%	15%	84%
71%	72%	92%	68%	85%	16%

Comparing Costs

Both sides spent approximately the same amount of money on the war, although costs were separated differently. However, due to the larger population in the North, the **per capita** cost there was far less—$148,000,000 to the South's $376,000,000.

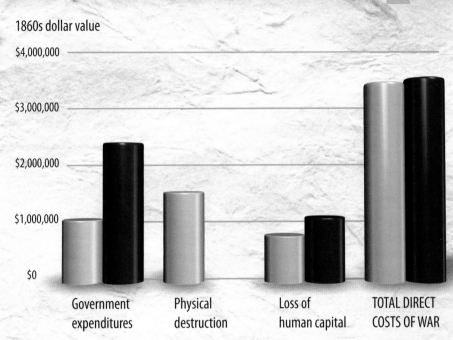

1860s dollar value

$4,000,000

$3,000,000

$2,000,000

$1,000,000

$0

Government expenditures

Physical destruction

Loss of human capital

TOTAL DIRECT COSTS OF WAR

North

South

The Human Cost of War

The North and South each lost a substantial number of soldiers during the war. Some died in battle, while others died later from their wounds. Many were taken by disease. Losses did not always mean death, however. Soldiers could be removed from battle by non-fatal wounds or as prisoners of war.

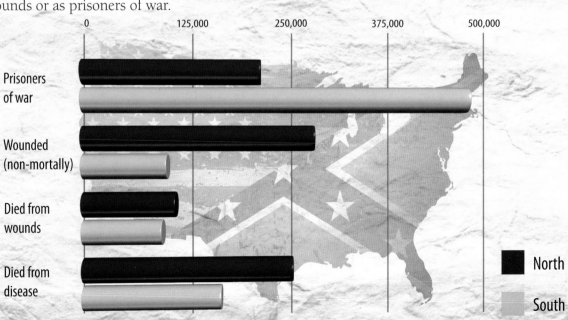

0   125,000   250,000   375,000   500,000

Prisoners of war

Wounded (non-mortally)

Died from wounds

Died from disease

North

South

Casualties of War

The Civil War was the deadliest war in American history. More soldiers lost their lives in the conflict than in all of the United States' other wars combined. This map indicates some of the Civil War's deadliest battles and the number of deaths for both sides in each.

The Deadliest Battles		Union	Confederate
1.	Gettysburg	23,000	28,000
2.	Chickamauga	16,170	18,454
3.	Spotsylvania Court House	18,000	12,000
4.	Wilderness	18,400	11,400
5.	Chancellorsville	17,304	13,460
6.	Shiloh	13,047	10,694
7.	Stones River	13,249	10,266
8.	Antietam	12,401	10,316
9.	Second Bull Run	13,830	8,350
10	Vicksburg	10,142	9,091
	Totals	155,543	132,031

Texas

Iowa

Pennsylvania

New Jersey

Ohio

Gettysburg, 1863

1

Indiana

8

Antietam, 1862

Illinois

9

Bull Run, 1862

Delaware

Maryland

5

Chancellorsville, 1863

4

Wilderness, 1864

Missouri

Kentucky

3

Virginia

Spotsylvania, 1864

North Carolina

Arkansas

Tennessee

7

Stones River, 1863

6

2

Chickamauga, 1863

Shiloh, 1862

South Carolina

Vicksburg, 1863

Alabama

Georgia

10

Mississippi

Louisiana

Florida

Legend

Union Army

Confederate Army

Neutral

Major Battle

0   250 Miles

N

0   250 Kilometers

How We Remember

The Civil War affected the country politically, economically, and socially. It also impacted people on a personal level. Many men did not return home from the war. Others returned with life-changing injuries. People wanted to honor those who had fought, those who had been injured, and those who had died throughout the course of the conflict.

GETTYSBURG NATIONAL CEMETERY

Gettysburg National Cemetery in located in Pennsylvania's Gettysburg National Military Park. It is the resting place for more than 3,500 Union soldiers who lost their lives in the Battle of Gettysburg. Veterans of other wars have also been buried at the site. There are a number of memorials in the area, including the Soldiers' National Monument, which was completed in 1869. The statue at the top of the monument is called the Genius of Liberty. It holds a wreath of peace in its right hand and a sword in the other. Around the base, marble statues represent History, Peace, Plenty, and War.

VICKSBURG NATIONAL MILITARY PARK

The Vicksburg National Military Park is found in the city of Vicksburg, Mississippi. This site of the 1863 battle is home to the Vicksburg National Cemetery, where approximately 17,000 Union soldiers are buried. The park has more than 1,300 monuments. The Louisiana Memorial is located at the highest point in the park. The 81-foot (24.7-m) tall column is topped with a granite sculpture of an eternal flame. The African American Soldier Memorial is also located in the Vicksburg National Military Park. Its three bronze figures commemorate African Americans who fought at Vicksburg.

SHILOH NATIONAL MILITARY PARK

Shiloh National Military Park in Tennessee is one of America's best-preserved battlefields and contains 151 monuments. The Confederate Monument is the largest and features a number of bronze statues that honor those who fought for the Confederacy. At 75 feet (22.9 m), the Iowa Memorial is one of the tallest monuments in the park. Honoring Iowan soldiers who died at the Battle of Shiloh, its base features a sculpture of a woman climbing the step to add an inscription. Shiloh National Cemetery is also contained within the park. More than 3,500 Union soldiers are buried there.

Memorials and other symbols of remembrance began to appear across the country in the decades after the Civil War. Some were local monuments, developed by individual communities. Others were created on behalf of the entire country and were sometimes combined with memorials dedicated to earlier conflicts. Today, these memorials and symbols continue to pay tribute to those who served in the Civil War.

THE PEACE MONUMENT

The Peace Monument is located on the grounds of the U.S. Capitol in Washington, DC. It is also known as the Naval Monument or the Civil War Sailors Monument. It commemorates those Americans who died at sea during the Civil War. Completed in early 1878, the monument is 44 feet (13.4 m) tall and made of white marble. Two statues stand at the top of the monument. Grief is depicted weeping on the shoulder of the statue representing History, who holds a tablet inscribed with the words, "They died that their country might live."

THE CONFEDERATE MEMORIAL

The Confederate Memorial is located in Arlington National Cemetery in Virginia. It honors the Confederate soldiers and sailors who died during the Civil War. The granite memorial is 32 feet (9.8 m) tall and is topped with a bronze statue of a woman, symbolizing the South. The statue's head is crowned with olive leaves to represent peace. Her left hand holds a laurel wreath in the direction of the South, acknowledging the soldiers' sacrifices. Her right hand rests on a plow, symbolizing the reconciliation between North and South after the war. Surrounding the memorial are the graves of Confederate soldiers.

THE CIVIL WAR UNKNOWNS MONUMENT

The Civil War Unknowns Monument is located on the grounds of Arlington House, the Robert E. Lee Memorial at Arlington National Cemetery in Virginia. The monument is 12 feet (3.7 m) tall and made of granite. It contains the remains of 2,111 unidentified soldiers from the battlefields of Bull Run and Rappahannock. It was the first monument at Arlington to be devoted to unknowns. Since it was very difficult to identify the bodies that were collected from the battlefields, it is assumed that the burial vault contains the remains of both Union and Confederate soldiers.

Test Yourself

MIX 'n MATCH

1. March to the Sea
2. Gettysburg Address
3. Fort Sumter
4. American Red Cross
5. Hornet's Nest
6. CSS *H. L. Hunley*
7. Pickett's Charge
8. Confederate president

a. Battle of Gettysburg
b. Battle of Shiloh
c. Submarine
d. William Tecumseh Sherman
e. Clara Barton
f. Jefferson Davis
g. North Carolina
h. Abraham Lincoln

TRUE OR FALSE

1. The Springfield rifle musket was the most widely used firearm of the war.

2. Richmond, Virginia was the capital city of the Confederacy.

3. The Thirteenth Amendment gave African Americans the right to vote.

4. The first shots of the war were fired at Fort Fisher, North Carolina.

5. At the start of the war, Union and Confederate soldiers were each paid $11 per month.

6. The Battle of Antietam was the bloodiest single day in American history.

7. Robert E. Lee was a commanding general for the Union Army.

8. When the war began, the Union Navy had more than 100 ships.

MULTIPLE CHOICE

1. When were the New York Draft Riots?
   a. September 1861
   b. November 1862
   c. July 1863
   d. April 1865

2. Which Civil War general later became president of the United States?
   a. Ulysses S. Grant
   b. Robert E. Lee
   c. William Tecumseh Sherman
   d. Stonewall Jackson

3. Where was Abraham Lincoln born?
   a. Indiana
   b. Virginia
   c. Kentucky
   d. Tennessee

4. Where did Robert E. Lee surrender his army in April 1865?
   a. Hampton Roads
   b. Appomattox Court House
   c. Fort Sumter
   d. Richmond

5. Who was put in charge of recruiting nurses for the Union Army?
   a. Dorothea Dix
   b. Frances Clayton
   c. Loreta Velazquez
   d. Clara Barton

6. How many cartridges did a soldier's cartridge box hold?
   a. 20
   b. 40
   c. 50
   d. 60

7. What finally abolished slavery in late 1865?
   a. The Emancipation Proclamation
   b. Reconstruction
   c. The Thirteenth Amendment
   d. The Gettysburg Address

Answers:
Mix and Match
1. d. 2. h. 3. g. 4. e. 5. b. 6. c. 7. a. 8. f
True or False
1. True 2. True 3. False 4. False 5. False 6. True 7. False 8. False
Multiple Choice
1. c. 2. a. 3. c. 4. b. 5. a. 6. b. 7. c.

The Civil War 45

Key Words

abolitionist: someone in favor of the abolition of slavery

ally: a country, group, or person in an alliance with another

artillery: large caliber weapons, such as cannons and howitzers

ballistics: relating to the flight of projectiles

blockade: the isolation of an area, usually a port, by ships to prevent entry and exit

casualties: people who have been lost after being killed, wounded, taken prisoner, or gone missing in action

cavalry: a section of an army that fights on horseback

colonial rule: when a nation maintains or extends its control over foreign dependencies

conscription: required enrolment in the armed forces, sometimes referred to as the draft

democracy: a form of government in which the supreme power is vested in the people and exercised directly by them or their elected representatives

dictators: people who rule absolutely and oppressively

impeached: charged with improper conduct

infantry: an army consisting of soldiers who fight on foot

infrastructure: facilities serving a country, such as transportation and communication systems

insignia: a badge or distinguishing mark of office or honor

March to the Sea: the name commonly given to the military campaign conducted through Georgia from November to December 1864

merchant marine: all of a country's ships that are used for trade and not war

offensive: an attack launched by military forces against the enemy

officers: people holding positions of authority in the military

per capita: for each person

rations: food supplies issued to a soldier or other member of the military

reconnaissance: the process of obtaining information about the position of the enemy

secede: to formally withdraw from membership in an organization

segregated: isolated or divided

snipers: soldiers who shoot at others from a concealed location

theaters: the entire land, sea, and air areas directly involved in war operations

Index

Log on to www.av2books.com

AV² by Weigl brings you media enhanced books that support active learning. Go to www.av2books.com, and enter the special code found on page 2 of this book. You will gain access to enriched and enhanced content that supplements and complements this book. Content includes video, audio, weblinks, quizzes, a slide show, and activities.

AV² Online Navigation

Audio
Listen to sections of the book read aloud.

Book Pages
AV² pages directly correspond to pages in the book.

Video
Watch informative video clips.

Key Words
Study vocabulary, and complete a matching word activity.

Embedded Weblinks
Gain additional information for research.

Try This!
Complete activities and hands-on experiments.

Quizzes
Test your knowledge.

Slide Show
View images and captions, and prepare a presentation.

AV² was built to bridge the gap between print and digital. We encourage you to tell us what you like and what you want to see in the future.

Sign up to be an AV² Ambassador at www.av2books.com/ambassador.